Sports Illustrated KIDS

STARS OF SPORTS

MIKAELA SHIFFRIN

OLYMPIC SKIING LEGEND

by *Mari Bolte*

CAPSTONE PRESS
a capstone imprint

Published by Capstone Press, an imprint of Capstone
1710 Roe Crest Drive, North Mankato, Minnesota 56003
capstonepub.com

Library of Congress Cataloging-in-Publication Data
Names: Bolte, Mari, author.
Title: Mikaela Shiffrin : Olympic skiing legend / by Mari Bolte.
Description: North Mankato, Minnesota : Capstone Press, 2024. | Series: Sports illustrated kids stars of sports | Includes bibliographical references and index. | Audience: Ages 8 to 11 | Audience: Grades 4-6 | Summary: "Raised in a skiing family, Mikaela Shiffrin seemed destined to be a skiing star from birth. In her very first Olympics, she became the youngest Olympic champion in her event. She would go on to compete in three more Olympic games. Learn about her journey to the Olympics, the challenges she faced, and how she has become an American Olympic skiing legend"— Provided by publisher.
Identifiers: LCCN 2022050201 (print) | LCCN 2022050202 (ebook) | ISBN 9781669018261 (hardcover) | ISBN 9781669018216 (paperback) | ISBN 9781669018223 (pdf) | ISBN 9781669018247 (kindle edition) | ISBN 9781669018254 (epub)
Subjects: LCSH: Shiffrin, Mikaela—Juvenile literature. | Skiers—United States—Biography—Juvenile literature. | Women skiers—United States—Biography—Juvenile literature. | Olympic athletes—United States—Biography—Juvenile literature. | Women Olympic athletes—United States—Biography—Juvenile literature.
Classification: LCC GV854.2.S46 B65 2024 (print) | LCC GV854.2.S46 (ebook) | DDC 796.93/5092 [B]—dc23/eng/20221020
LC record available at https://lccn.loc.gov/2022050201
LC ebook record available at https://lccn.loc.gov/2022050202

Editorial Credits
Editor: Mandy Robbins; Designer: Hilary Wacholz; Media Researcher: Jo Miller; Production Specialist: Tori Abraham

Image Credits
Alamy: Action Plus Sports Images, 28, REUTERS, 15, ZUMA Press, Inc., 23; Getty Images: Adam Pretty, 25, Alexis Boichard/Agence Zoom, 5, Christophe Pallot/Agence Zoom, 13, 17, 19, Simon Bruty, 9, TIZIANA FABI, 20, Tom Pennington, 7, 27; Newscom: Maxim Thore/ZUMAPRESS, cover; Shutterstock: action sports, 14, Martynova Anna, 1, Roman Malanchuk, 16, Salty View, 24, Steve Boice, 8; Sports Illustrated/Erick W. Rasco, 11, 21

Source Notes
Pg. 6: "They had us walking around . . ." Áine Cain, "How to Raise an Olympian, According to the Parents of Gold Medalist Mikaela Shiffrin," *Business Insider*, February 15, 2018, https://www.businessinsider.com/how-to-raise-olympian-mikaela-shiffrin-2018-2, accessed July 4, 2022.
Pg. 8: "I don't have . . ." Tim Layden, "Young, Gifted, and Oh So Fast," *Sports Illustrated*, https://www.si.com/longform/sochi/shiffrin/index.html, accessed July 22, 2022.
Pg. 10: "She was doing things . . ." Meg Noonan, "Becoming Mikaela," *Yankee Magazine*, January 2020, https://newengland.com/yankee-magazine/living/profiles/alpine-skier-mikaela-shiffrin/, accessed July 22, 2022.
Pg. 12: "They've all told me . . ." Brian Pinelli, "10 Years Ago Today, 16-Year-Old Mikaela Shiffrin Made Her World Cup Debut," *Ski Magazine,* March 11, 2021, https://www.skimag.com/athletes/racers/mikaela-shiffrin-world-cup-debut/, accessed July 22, 2022.
Pg. 15: "Everyone keeps bringing up Sochi . . ." Bill Pennington, "American, 17, Wins in Slalom an dMakes Herself a Favorite in Sochi," *The New York Times*, February 16, 2013, https://www.nytimes.com/2013/02/17/sports/world-champion-at-17-american-wins-in-Slalom.html, accessed July 22, 2022.
Pg. 21: "There were moments . . ." Barry Svrluga, "Mikaela Shiffrin Snaps Out of Her Recent Slump and Puts Olympics on Notice," *The Washington Post*, February 15, 2018, https://www.washingtonpost.com/sports/olympics/mikaela-shiffrin-snaps-out-of-her-recent-slump-and-puts-olympics-on-notice/2018/02/15/5dac20b0-121f-11e8-9570-29c9830535e5_story.html, accessed July 22, 2022.
Pg. 24: "It has to be gold . . ." *Europsort*, "Winter Olympics 2022 – Mikaela Shiffrin Admits Games is a 'Pretty Stressful and Uncomfortable' Experience," *Eurosport*, February 2, 2022, https://www.eurosport.com/alpine-skiing/beijing-2022/2022/winter-olympics-2022-shiffrin-admits-olympic-games-is-a-pretty-stressful-and-uncomfortable-experienc_sto8749603/story.shtml, accessed July 21, 2022.
Pg. 26: "I felt the pressure . . ." Rose Minutaglio, "Mikaela Shiffrin Lost the Olympics But Won the World," *ELLE*, July 18, 2022, https://www.elle.com/culture/a40478203/mikaela-shiffrin-olympics-skier/, accessed July 21, 2022.
Pg. 28: "I'm also proud . . ." Bill Pennington, "With a Fourth World Cup Overall Title, Mikaela Shiffrin is Back on Top," *The New York Times*, March 17, 2022, https://www.nytimes.com/2022/03/17/sports/skiing/shiffrin-world-cup-olympics.html, accessed July 22, 2022.

All internet sites appearing in back matter were available and accurate when this book was sent to press.

TABLE OF CONTENTS

Words in **BOLD** are in the glossary.

SLIDING INTO THE OLYMPICS

Mikaela Shiffrin crouched at the top of a snowy hill in Russia. Warning beeps sounded in her ears. She pushed off hard. Her legs hit the electric timer on the way out of the starting box. Her second Olympic **slalom** run had begun.

It was Shiffrin's first Olympics. The snow wasn't ideal. Shiffrin also had a cold. But nothing slowed her down. Her first slalom run had been nearly flawless. She had finished the course 0.49 seconds faster than her nearest competitor.

The second run started smoothly. She wove between the flexible red and blue slalom **gates**. Suddenly, halfway through the course, she bobbled and nearly crashed. But Shiffrin righted herself. She kept on going. And she became the youngest Olympic slalom champion!

〉〉〉 Shiffrin competing in the
2014 Sochi Olympics

CHAPTER ONE

BORN TO SKI

Mikaela Shiffrin was born in Vail, Colorado, on March 13, 1995 to Jeff Shiffrin and Eileen Shiffrin. Jeff was a doctor, and Eileen was a nurse. Mikaela has an older brother named Taylor.

The Shiffrins loved to ski. Jeff had skied in college for Dartmouth. Eileen competed in Adult, or Masters, racing. As soon as their children could stand, they taught them to ski.

"They had us walking around in the living room in these tiny, little, plastic Mickey Mouse skis that you just latched onto snow boots," Taylor said later. Shiffrin still remembers skiing down their driveway when she was 2 years old.

>>> Shiffrin's parents, Eileen and Jeff, pose with her after her 2017 FIS championship.

Ski Colorado

Colorado is famous for its ski towns. Aspen and Vail are the most well-known. Telluride, Winter Park, and Breckenridge are also popular. More than 300 inches (762 centimeters) of snow falls on Colorado's Rocky Mountains every year. The weather is also mild and sunny, making Colorado ideal for lovers of the outdoors.

At about 7 years old, Shiffrin entered an after-school ski program at Vail Ski Resort. Her parents' jobs and skiing backgrounds allowed her and Taylor the privilege of learning at one of the most expensive resorts in the country.

Early on, the skiing instructors watched the children ski as best they could. Then they would put the children into training groups. Most kids were nervous. They slowly **snowplowed** down the hill. Not Shiffrin! Her parents had already taught her to make fast, smooth arcs in the snow. When she reached the bottom, the instructor looked at her and said, "I don't have a group for you."

⟩⟩⟩ Skiers flock to the slopes in Vail, Colorado.

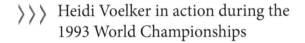

>>> Heidi Voelker in action during the
1993 World Championships

When Shiffrin was 6 years old, she got Olympic
skier Heidi Voelker's autograph. Voelker added
"ABFTTB." It stood for "Always be faster than
the boys." Shiffrin began using it as her motto.

Shiffrin consistently impressed coaches. "She was doing things as an 8-year-old that most kids didn't start to learn until years later," one coach remembered. "That came from a lot of hours on snow." She was also known for her good attitude and strong focus.

When Shiffrin was 11, the family moved to New England. Taylor went to an expensive **prep school** in Vermont called Burke Mountain Academy. It trained future professional ski racers. Shiffrin was being home schooled. In the afternoon, she trained with the prep school racers.

FACT

Shiffrin was the second-youngest U.S. skier to ever win at the World Cup level.

At 13, Shiffrin and her parents moved back to Vail. Taylor stayed in Vermont. Shiffrin missed the competitive school. She missed her friends and coaches there. She was so homesick that she no longer wanted to train. Alarmed, her parents let her return to Burke. Within three months, Shiffrin became an international champion.

〉〉〉 In 2016, Shiffrin competed in Vermont for the 2016 FIS World Cup.

By 2011, Shiffrin had competed in her first World Cup race. At almost 16, she was the youngest competitor. There she met top racers, including Lindsey Vonn and Maria Riesch. "They've all told me that I could ask them anything," she told a reporter for *Ski Magazine*. Her energy inspired the older skiers. It made them remember why they loved competing.

That December, Shiffrin won her first World Cup medal. She took third place in slalom in Lienz, Austria. Her first gold was earned the next year at the age of 17.

Through the Gates

There are six Alpine World Cup skiing events. Mikaela usually specializes in two: slalom and giant slalom.

In slalom, the gates are close together and the turns are fast. With giant slalom, the hill is steeper. There are many gates and turns. Both are **technical** events. Usually, skiers get two tries. Then the times are combined.

Speed events only allow one shot at the course. The hills are much steeper, and the number of gates depends on the course. Downhill speeds can reach 100 miles (161 kilometers) per hour.

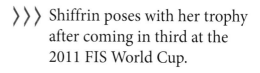

>>> Shiffrin poses with her trophy after coming in third at the 2011 FIS World Cup.

CHAPTER THREE

UPS AND DOWNS

In 2012, Shiffrin joined the U.S. Ski Team. Athletes are selected based on their performance and ranking. They represent the United States at the World Cup, World Championship, and Olympic level.

>>> Shiffrin competing in giant slalom on November 29, 2012

Shiffrin became a world champion in 2013. At 17 years old, she was the youngest woman to win the slalom title since 1985. She was a favorite for the upcoming Sochi Winter Olympics. But she didn't let the pressure get to her. "Everyone keeps bringing up Sochi to me," she said. "But it is a long way away . . . I'm focused on right now."

In Sochi, Shiffrin took the top combined time in her slalom runs and won the gold. She was the youngest ever Olympic slalom champion. People called her the "Princess of the 2014 Sochi Winter Games."

〉〉〉 Shiffrin on the podium after winning gold in the slalom event at the 2014 Sochi Olympics

Returning to ordinary life can be hard after competing in the Olympics. Shiffrin just kept enjoying racing. She ended the 2014–15 season with more wins. She broke world records. Shiffrin also attended a training camp in Italy. She tried out new equipment too.

>>> Marlies Schild (left), Mikaela Shiffrin (center), and Kathrin Zettel (right) pose with their hardware after the women's alpine skiing slalom at Sochi 2014 XXII Olympic Winter Games.

Shiffrin faced a big change the next year at 20 years old. Her mother had traveled with her since she began racing. But Eileen wanted to go back to being a nurse. Shiffrin would have to travel alone.

Shiffrin's first race without her family was in Åre, Sweden, in December 2015. Eileen watched Mikaela on TV. She saw her take a hard fall during warm-ups. It injured her right knee. Mikaela missed most of the rest of the season.

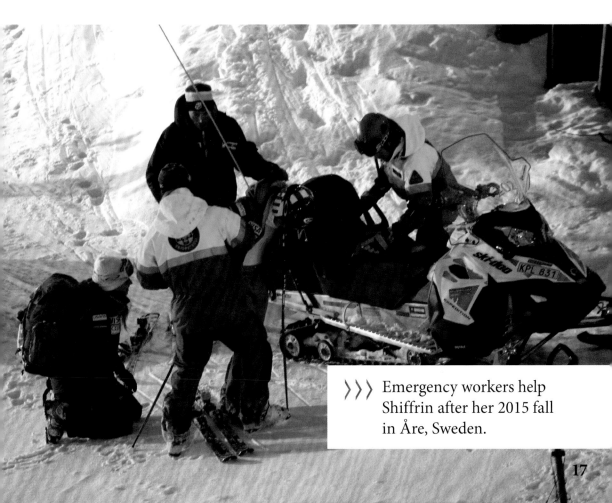

〉〉〉 Emergency workers help Shiffrin after her 2015 fall in Åre, Sweden.

CHAPTER FOUR

TITLES TO WIN AND DEFEND

Shiffrin returned to the ski hill in February 2016. She won seven slalom races in a row that season. She also won her first World Cup overall title.

The 2016 Audi FIS Ski World Cup season took place across 74 races at 29 different hills. Each race awarded points to the top 30 winners. At the end of each season, the skier with the most points in each event and overall wins a crystal globe. Shiffrin won her first globe that year. She was just 22. People were calling her the best skier in the world.

FACT

The Alpine Skiing World Cup in Levi, Finland, awards winners live reindeer. Shiffrin has won four. Their names are Ingemar, Rudolph, Mr. Gru, and Sven. They live in Finland.

>>> Shiffrin poses with her reindeer after winning the Audi FIS Alpine Ski World Cup Women's Slalom on November 17. 2018 in Levi, Finland.

Shiffrin's 2017–18 season was tough. She felt pressure to defend her titles. She also wanted to collect more medals. Technical events had been her specialty. Now, she pushed herself in speed events too.

In January, Shiffrin entered the super-G in Cortina, Italy. Super-G is a longer course than regular giant slalom. The hill is steeper too. It was only the fourth time she had entered that event. She hoped to add more World Cup points to her tally. Unfortunately, wind conditions were not ideal. Shiffrin did not finish (DNF). Her next five races were seventh places and DNFs.

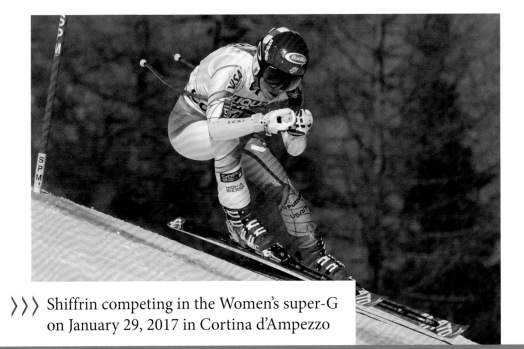

⟩⟩⟩ Shiffrin competing in the Women's super-G on January 29, 2017 in Cortina d'Ampezzo

Shiffrin decided to take a break before the 2018 PyeongChang Winter Olympics. She showed up refreshed. But her nerves had always been her biggest enemy. "There were moments where I thought, 'I don't know if I'm good enough to do this,'" she admitted. She overcame them, though, winning a gold and a silver medal.

⟩⟩⟩ Shiffrin in action during the 2018 PyeongChang Winter Olympics

Shiffrin's 2018–2019 season was impressive. She won 17 races. She also became the first ski racer to win gold in all six **Alpine** ski events.

Shiffrin ended her season winning the slalom at the FIS Alpine World Ski Championships in Sweden. She won a World Cup Championship title for the third year in a row. That hadn't been done since 1939, by German skier Christi Cranz.

In October 2019, Shiffrin's life took a sad turn. Her grandmother died. The two had been close. Tragedy struck again on February of 2020. Her father fell in an accident. Shiffrin and Eileen were in Italy when it happened. The family was able to be together before Jeff passed away on February 2.

FACT

The Jeff Shiffrin Athlete **Resiliency** Fund was set up in 2020. It gives money to help athletes with training or competition costs. It also helps with living or medical expenses.

>>> Shiffrin with her dad, Jeff, in 2020

Soon after her father's death, the **COVID-19 pandemic** began. Shiffrin tested positive for the **virus** late in 2021. Then in October, back pain forced her to take a break. Preparing for the 2022 Beijing Winter Olympics was not going well.

CHAPTER FIVE

THE BEIJING WINTER OLYMPICS

Shiffrin struggled in the lead-up to the Beijing Winter Olympics. But she was still favored to win at least one gold medal. The pressure was on.

Shiffrin had watched gymnast Simone Biles during the Tokyo Olympics in 2020. Like Shiffrin, Biles had been expected to sweep the competition. But Biles withdrew due to mental health struggles. Shiffrin understood the pressure Biles was going through. She told reporters, "It has to be gold or else that's a huge disappointment. It even went a step beyond that. It wouldn't have been a 'disappointment,' people didn't even consider it a possibility. And what I know from that kind of pressure is: It is not easy to win. Ever."

〉〉〉 Simone Biles

>>> Shiffrin, after a disappointing run at the 2022 Olympics

Experts said Shiffrin could win up to five gold medals in Beijing. But she ended her third Olympic games without a single one. She crashed in three races. Mikaela was frustrated. "I felt the pressure, disappointment, shame, and embarrassment of knowing I couldn't go back and change it," she later said.

Shiffrin was never able to explain what happened during her runs. Something had just been off that day. She braced herself for sharp criticism. But it never came.

Support from teammates, fans, and fellow athletes poured in. They sent Shiffrin words of encouragement. Shiffrin felt like she had let down her teammates. But they let her know that she was more than a medal.

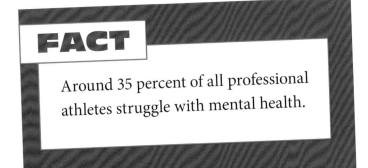

FACT

Around 35 percent of all professional athletes struggle with mental health.

Despite her disappointment, Shiffrin did accomplish something important. She became just the second woman to race in six Winter Olympics events.

〉〉〉 Shiffrin wipes out during the 2022 Beijing Olympics.

After the Olympics, Shiffrin said she had a little embarrassment. But then she said, "I'm also proud that I got back up and raced and never stopped trying."

She finished her 2022 season with her fourth World Cup crystal globe in the women's all-around. She tied Lindsey Vonn for the American record. Only one other woman, Austrian Annemarie Moser-Proll, has more, with six total.

Shiffrin has learned from her successes and failures. And she has not let her Olympic performance stop her. There are many more world records within her reach. And she's ready for wherever the future takes her.

〉〉〉 Shiffrin poses with one of her many FIS Alpine Ski championship globes.

TIMELINE

1995 Mikaela Shiffrin is born on March 13 in Vail, Colorado.

2001 Mikaela tries out for an after-school ski program.

2003 The Shiffrin family moves to New England.

2011 Shiffrin competes in her first World Cup race.

2012 Shiffrin joins the U.S. Ski Team.

2014 Shiffrin competes in the Sochi Olympics, winning a gold medal in slalom.

2016 Shiffrin wins her first women's overall crystal globe.

2018 Shiffrin wins one gold medal and one silver medal during the PyeongChang Olympics.

2020 Jeff Shiffrin dies in an accident.

2022 Shiffrin competes at the Beijing Olympics.

GLOSSARY

ALPINE (AL-pyn)—relating to high mountains

COVID-19 PANDEMIC (KOH-vid nine-TEEN pan-DEM-ik)—a very contagious, sometimes deadly, virus that spread worldwide in 2020

GATE (GATE)—a narrow pole with a flag attached; slalom racers carve around gates

PREP SCHOOL (PREP SKOOL)—a private school that prepares students for the future

RESILIENCY (ruh-ZILL-yuhn-see)—the ability to recover quickly from challenges

SLALOM (SLAH-luhm)—an individual Alpine race around obstacles

SNOWPLOW (SNOW-plow)—a simple way of turning or stopping; the points of the skis are turned in toward each other

TECHNICAL (TEK-ni-kuhl)—specialized

VIRUS (VYE-ruhss)—a germ that infects living things and causes diseases

READ MORE

Gish, Ashley. *Alpine Skiing*. Mankato, MN: Creative Education, 2022.

Gitlin, Marty. *Lindsey Vonn: Olympic Ski Champion*. New York: Britannica Educational Publishing, in association with Rosen Educational Services, 2019.

Herman, Gail. *What Are the Winter Olympics?* New York: Penguin Workshop, 2021.

Price, Karen. *GOATs of Olympic Sports*. North Mankato, MN: SportsZone, an imprint of Abdo Publishing, 2022.

INTERNET SITES

Olympics: Alpine Skiing
olympics.com/en/sports/alpine-skiing/

Team USA: Mikaela Shiffrin
teamusa.org/us-ski-and-snowboard/athletes/mikaela-shiffrin

U.S. Ski Team: Mikaela Shiffrin
usskiandsnowboard.org/athletes/mikaela-shiffrin

INDEX

AUTHOR BIO

Mari Bolte is the author and editor of many books for children, ranging from video games to cute animals to sports stars. She grew up skiing and has also spent time as a ski race parent.